AN ANGLER'S
TO THE SOUL

Ron Smith

ARTHUR H. STOCKWELL LTD.
Elms Court   Ilfracombe
Devon

© Ron Smith, 1983
First published in Great Britain, 1983

In memory of my father, Victor Smith, himself a fine angler, whose example I have always tried to copy.

ACKNOWLEDGEMENTS

A special thanks to the Tackle Shops for their co-operation and help with sales of my last book, also to my wife who kindly did the illustrations.

ISBN 0 7223 1754-9
Printed in Great Britain by
Arthur H. Stockwell Ltd.
Elms Court   Ilfracombe
Devon

CONTENTS

Introduction	5
Part I	
Places to Fish (Sea)	11
Part II	
Places to Fish (Freshwater)	31
Part III	
Stories and Tackle Tips	37
Part IV	
Inshore Boat-Fishing Marks	55
Part V	
Your Bait and Where to Find It	59
Part VI	
Your Fish and Where to Find Them	63
Part VII	
A General Guide to Shore Fishing in the West Country	73
Part VIII	
The Effect of Weather Conditions	77
Part IX	
Maps	81
Part X	
Quizwords	89

INTRODUCTION

This is a guide to sea angling in the West Country. It describes the species which can be caught and the best baits to use. All these places I have fished many times.

I was introduced to the sport of angling by my father, also a keen angler. I started at the age of 14 — 22 years ago — so have been fishing for a very long time. I am truly a dedicated angler and fish all the year round.

At the end of a working week, what better way of relaxing than a few hours' fishing. The West Country is an angling paradise, whether for sea fishing or freshwater. In the estuaries for flounder or bass; off the rocks for the hard-fighting wrasse; perhaps river fishing for the king — the salmon — or try your hand at reservoir fishing for rainbow trout.

Some would say an angler is lucky if he catches a fish, but an angler who can consistently catch fish is never a lucky angler. He studies the weather and tides; he knows when to fish and when not to fish; he will make sure he has the right bait and take the trouble to dig worms or collect crabs himself. A good angler will be an all-year-round angler, who will derive a great sense of satisfaction returning home with a bag of specimen fish. Some day he may even break a record; perhaps the flounder or wrasse record — both seem far from being safe — or maybe a specimen small-eyed ray will find his anchored sand-eel. An angler lives in a world of his own, spending many hours alone on the rocks, perhaps at night, with only the occasional cry of a seagull or the lapping of the waves for company.

Fishing is like a drug: catch a few fish and you will be hooked for life. My first fish was a mullet of hardly five inches long, but no amount of money could buy it.

The West Country has some superb fishing to offer, even in this age of increased gill-netting. There are some fabulous marks (some have never seen a baited hook), places where giant wrasse and bass roam. 'Explore the coastline' is the only answer, and when you have found a good place, then — with angling increasing day by day — it pays to keep it to yourself or that place will soon be fished out. Some dedicated anglers use ropes down the cliffs to help them get to their favourite mark; perhaps the coastline between Stoke and Mothecombe, or from Bovisand, Heybrook Bay to the Wembury area. They have some very deep gullies and a few sandy beaches between them; a survey at low water would show up the bottom clearly.

Remember: return all immature fish — bass, rays, wrasse, whatever the species — fish stocks are diminishing fast. Take only what you need and be conservation minded. The mackerel is another threatened species; you only have to look at the size on sale in the shops. The bigger ones are few and far between.

ENJOY YOUR FISHING!

Ron Smith.

A favourite mark between Stoke Point and Mothecombe.

Polperro.

A good rock mark between Stoke Point and Mothecombe.

Plaice 2-15oz. — caught at my favourite mark on king ragworm — 1982.

Wrasse 6lb.8oz. — caught at Stoke Beach on peeler crab — 1982.

Giant wrasse 7lb.4oz. — caught on large peeler crab — 1982.

PART I

PLACES TO FISH (SEA)

PLACES TO FISH (SEA)

Slapton
This place fishes best after dark on a flood tide when there is a very good depth of water close in. A cast of some 50 or 60 yards will land in up to 30 feet of water. Use worm baits for a variety of species and fish baits for dogfish. Weed can be troublesome after a storm. There is good parking close by.

East Portlemouth (nr. Salcombe)
A good mark for bass, mullet, pouting, whiting, flounder, dabs, plaice, rockling, wrasse and pollack. Fishing is best after dark on the flood or ebb tide — the last hour of the ebb is particularly good. Use ledger gear and cast beyond the third breaker, some 100 yards out, and fish near the freshwater stream. Bait with king ragworm or lugworm.

Bantham
Fished best on the flood tide, two hours before high water; preferably a spring tide. Weed can be bad after a storm. Best bait is lugworm, but fish can be caught on king ragworm — notably bass and the occasional dab. Easy parking close by.

Thurlestone Sands
Fish the beach near the freshwater river for bass, plaice, pouting, rockling, conger and occasionally red mullet. Best

baits are lugworm, king ragworm and sand-eel. Fishing is best at night. Weed can be troublesome at times after a period of rough weather.

Bigbury (Burgh Island)
Wrasse, rockling and spider crabs (in season) can be caught on the flood or ebb tide. Best baits to use are worm or fish strip. Good parking in the main car park (which charged 50p at the time of going to press).

Wembury Rocks
Wrasse are taken on the flood tide but are mainly on the small side. School bass are occasionally caught from the main beach. Use worm baits and sliding float tackle for wrasse; use ledger tackle on the beach for bass. Lugworm and sand-eel can be dug on the beach. Easy parking.

Wembury Point
Fish the gullies for wrasse and spider crabs (in season) using worm or fish strip. Fish the flood tide. A bad bottom in places, so be prepared to lose tackle. Good parking space here.

Heybrook Bay
This is big wrasse country. A good depth of water in some of the gullies. Best to fish ledger tackle, but a very bad bottom so be prepared to lose a lot of gear. Small pollack can be taken after dark on float tackle. Spider crabs in season — but use fish baits. For wrasse use worm or limpet. Fishing is best on spring tides.

Bovisand Rocks
Fish for wrasse, pollack and mullet — sometimes spider crabs in summer. Fish the flood tide, using worm baits and float tackle. Easy fishing and good parking close by.

Bovisand Pier
Big wrasse, bass, pollack and occasional John Dorys are caught on worm baits. Fish the flood tide (preferably a spring tide). Pouting are caught at night. Lugworm can be dug on the spot.

A rocky bottom with a few sand patches. Fish from the wall about 30 feet up from the water. A drop net is advisable.

The Embankment (Laira)
Fishes best at night on the flood tide. School bass, mullet and the occasional thornback ray can be caught on worm bait. Eels and good sized flounders can be caught after dark. Good parking on the road.

Maristow (Lopwell Dam)
Good sized flounders, school bass, mullet and eels. The occasional sole may be taken using worm baits, lugworm or small ragworm. Fish the flood tide (springs are preferable to neaps). Fish by the old boat-house or on the grass bank where the river bends. You can also fish off the wall next to the water-mill. Fish in daylight as eels are a menace after dark. Good fishing and parking.

Blaxton Quay
Small school bass and eels can be caught on the flood tide using worm baits. Walk along a narrow path from Lopwell through the woods. Crabs can be troublesome. Limited parking in the road near Lopwell.

Seventeen Arches
Found by following the path about half a mile up river from Blaxton Quay. Good sport with nice sized bass; also flounders close to 3 lb have been taken at times. Big mullet roam around the bridge supports and are caught on light float tackle using tiny ragworm as bait. Fish the flood or ebb tide — springs are usually best.

Warleigh Point
Big bass can be caught on spring tides (my personal best at this mark is 8 lb 1 oz), also flounders and eels. In winter, whiting and pouting can be caught. Use worm baits. Very strong currents run on spring tides; a fair amount of lead is needed at times. Crabs can be troublesome. Deep water close in; a cast of only 40 to 50 yards will land in the main channel.

Ernsettle Creek (nr. bridge)
Fish the flood or ebb tide for school bass, flounders, plaice, eels, whiting, pouting and pollack in winter. Fish after dark for whiting and pouting. Use worm baits or fish strips in winter.

Tamerton Creek
Fish the flood or ebb tide for school bass, mullet and eels. Use lugworm or ragworm. Crabs are a menace during the summer months while the water is warm. Easy fishing. Good parking in the road.

Ernsettle Point
Fair sized bass are caught at times (some up to 7 lb have been taken), also flounder, mullet, eel, whiting, pouting and the occasional pollack. Use worm bait or fish baits after dark in winter. Fish the flood or ebb on spring tides.

Ernsettle (Bay)
Best fishing is on the last two hours of the flood tide. Fish alongside a small overflow pipe for school bass, flounders, pouting and whiting. Occasional eels can also be taken. Worm bait or prawns are good.

Ernsettle (nr. Platelayers Hut)
Bass, flounder, pouting, whiting and eels can be taken from this spot. Fishes best on the flood tide. Use king ragworm or lugworm; both can be dug on the spot. Easy fishing.

Ernsettle (Rock Pile)
Good fishing for flounder, bass, whiting and eels. Flood tides are best, preferably springs. Use king ragworm, lugworm or peeler crab. Good fishing — especially after dark.

Mud Cott Creek
Fishes quite well for school bass, flounder, whiting, pouting and eels. Fish the flood or ebb tide, preferably after dark, on springs. Use worm or soft crab baits. Easy fishing and parking in the road.

Wearde Quay
Fishes best after dark on the flood or ebb tide for school bass, flounders, whiting, pouting and eels. Use worm baits and cast well out. Crabs can be troublesome at times. Easy fishing but limited parking in the road.

Halton Quay
Large eels can be caught on worm baits, also flounders and occasional school bass. Fish the flood tide in daylight; fast currents run on spring tides. Easy fishing, and parking on the spot.

Landulph Point
Flounders can be caught on worm bait, but crabs make life difficult. Fish the flood tide; very deep water even at low tide. Eels can be caught at night. Big mullet roam close to the rocks; small school bass work their way up the creek. Use worm baits or peeler crab. Limited parking, in the road by the farm gate.

Portwrinkle
To the left of Finneygook Beach about 150 yards across the rocks, there is a point where bass, turbot, mackerel and pouting (after dark) can be caught. Best on spring tides. Use worm baits (mackerel strip or sand-eel for turbot). Be prepared to spend at least 7 hours on these rocks until the tide drops. Easy parking in the main car park.

Finneygook Beach
A good beach for dabs, plaice, mackerel and pouting at night. Fish the flood tide on springs — 2 hours before high water is the best time. Cast beyond the third breaker. Use worm baits, but mackerel strip for mackerel.

Seaton Beach
A very good beach at times. Big bass are caught here, most of them after dark. Fish up to 13 lb have been caught here, but some degree of dedication is needed. Good fishing on the third or fourth tide after a storm. Also conger, plaice, pouting and whiting at night, and the occasional scad

mackerel on fish baits. Good parking on the road.

Rusty Anchor
Another good spot with very deep water close in. Big bass, pollack, wrasse, pouting and conger after dark; a rocky bottom that hides many species. Use worm baits or squid and mackerel fillets if you are after conger. The flood tide is best, but very strong currents run on spring tides.

Western Kings (Hard Standing)
Float fish for pollack, wrasse and rockling, as the bottom is very rocky. Fishable only on neap tides as very strong currents run on springs. Use king ragworm or lugworm. Good parking space in the car park.

Millbay Docks
Good fishing for many species. There are many jetties and piers to fish from. Bass, flounder, brill, mackerel, garfish, wrasse, pollack, mullet, conger and pouting at night. Fish the flood or ebb tide and use king ragworm, lugworm, mackerel strip, squid or prawn. You will need a fishing permit, obtainable on application at the office just inside the entrance. A fee is payable, which was £9 at time of going to press.

Richmond Walk
Fish alongside the marina for bass, mullet, flounder, pouting, whiting and eels. Best after dark on the flood tide; fishes best on springs. Use king ragworm or lugworm. Very good size pouting are caught here, many over a pound. Parking on the spot.

Admiral's Hard
Excellent fishing at times. Good bags are taken, mainly at night. One of the few places that will fish best on the ebb tide, and springs are best. Use lugworm or king ragworm for school bass, flounder, rockling and pouting at night, and occasional eels. Parking on the waste ground close by.

Stoke Beach
Fish the flood tide from the first beach at night for conger,

using mackerel, squid or bunched ragworm. A rough bottom, so expect to lose tackle.

Stoke Point
A fantastic mark. Huge wrasse, many up to seven pounds, also bass, pollack and pouting at night. Big mullet roam close to the rocks and will take tiny ragworm or bread. Use a small quill float. Use king ragworm or crab for wrasse. Fishes best on the flood tide. A good place to spin for pollack and bass.

Steer Point (River Yealm)
Good sized whiting are caught here in winter and at night, but crabs are a menace. You can also catch eels after dark. Fish the flood tide. Use king ragworm or lugworm. Ragworm can be dug on the spot. Limited parking in the road.

North Corner, Devonport
Fish at night on the flood tide for pouting, whiting and dabs. Fish from the pontoon using worm baits. Very deep water close in. A very popular mark and it is very heavily fished. Parking close to the pontoon.

Pottery Quay, Devonport
Good fishing for bass, pollack, small wrasse and occasional thornback ray. At night, whiting and pouting, and during a very cold spell cod can be caught. Use worm or peeler crab. Fish the flood or ebb tide. Another very popular spot. Parking on the spot.

Barbican (Phoenix Wharf)
Fish the flood or ebb tide for bass, wrasse, pollack, mackerel, garfish, plaice; and after dark whiting, pouting and conger. Use worm baits, crab or mackerel and squid fillets for conger. A very popular spot and heavily fished. An easy place to fish and plenty of parking space.

Plymouth Hoe Rocks
Fish at night for pouting, rockling and conger. There are many caves close in holding deep water where conger hide. Fish for them using mackerel fillets and squid, and worm baits

for pouting. An easy place to fish, and parking on the main road close by.

Mutton Cove
Fish for wrasse, mullet, pouting; and after dark pollack can be caught on float tackle under the light of a tilley, using king ragworm or lugworm. Mackerel venture close to the pier during the summer months. Conger roam at night and will go for mackerel, herring or squid strips. A very popular place during the summer months. Parking in the road close to the pier.

Tregantle Beach (Whitsands)
Fair sport with bass, plaice, dabs and pouting. Cast beyond the third breaker on a flood tide. Fishes best at night. Use king ragworm or lugworm. A hard climb down the cliffs. Park in the lay-by at the cliff top.

Wilcove Pontoon
Bass, thornback ray and — after dark — pouting are caught here. Use worm baits, or if you are after ray, crab or mackerel fillets. Fish the flood tide. Strong currents run on high springs. A very bad bottom and a lot of gear is lost; cast well out into the main channel. A very popular mark during the day or at night. Limited parking space close to the pontoon.

Brunel Green
To the left of the bridge, Saltash side. Fair sport with school bass, flounder and large eels. Fish the flood or ebb tide and use worm baits. Strong currents run on spring tides. Cast well out. Parking close by on the road.

Challaborough Rocks
If you like catching pouting then this is the place. Very deep water. Fish the flood tide in daylight or darkness, it doesn't really matter which. Use worm baits or squid strips. Weed can be troublesome. You must be prepared to spend up to 7 hours on these rocks, until the tide drops enough to get back across the beach. A very popular place in the summer, so limited parking.

Camel's Head
A good place for school bass and mullet. Fish the flood tide; springs are best. Use lugworm or tiny ragworm. Park in the side roads close by.

Harlyn Bay, nr. Padstow
Fish from the high cliff, casting across the beach, using sand-eel or lugworm for bass, and mackerel are caught on feathers or by spinning. Very deep water. Fishes best on the flood tide. A drop net would be an advantage as you will be fishing some 30 feet up from the water. Parking at the caravan site.

Picklecombe Pier
Produces very little, but fair sized rockling. Use worm baits. A very bad bottom. Best to float fish. You must get permission to fish here as the pier is inside the fort. Very deep water here, and plenty of parking space.

Laira Bridge
Fair fishing for school bass and flounder, with small pouting and whiting at night. Fish the flood or ebb tide using king ragworm, lugworm or garden worms. Crabs can be troublesome. Limited parking close by the bridge.

Coypool
Many species make their way up this river with the flood tide: school bass, mullet, eels. Use garden worms or small ragworm. Eels are a menace after dark when salmon and sea trout make their way up. Parking space by the old iron bridge.

Tregonhawke Beach
You must cast beyond the third breaker here to catch bass and flat-fish. After dark is the best time, on a flood tide. Springs are best. Some very big bass have been caught from this beach. Use worm or sand-eel. A rather difficult climb down to this beach and limited parking on the road.

Cattedown Wharves
Fish alongside one of the overflow pipes and you will be in with

a chance of catching mullet, which feed on tiny scraps that come from them. Use a small quill float and bread or tiny ragworm. Small pouting sometimes caught after dark. Use ragworm or lugworm. Fish the flood or ebb tide. Parking close by in the road near the railway lines.

Stonehouse Creek
Fish the early flood for school bass, mullet, eels and occasional flounder. Use king ragworm or lugworm. Crabs can be troublesome. Whiting after dark during winter, after a period of hard frost. Parking close by in the road.

Point Beach, Saltram
Fish the flood tide using ragworm, lugworm or garden worm for school bass and mullet. Best on spring tides. Crabs make life difficult. Parking close by in the lay-by.

Bull Point
Fish the flood tide using worm baits for school bass and flounder. Eels can be troublesome after dark until a period of hard frost drives them out into deeper water. Whiting can be caught after dark in winter. Fast currents run on spring tides. Fish to the left of the pier, casting on the mud flats. Plenty of parking space near the bridge.

Shillingham Point
A useful mark for flounders. Fish the flood tide and use lugworm or ragworm. A fair walk to this point through Shillingham Farm, but keep to the footpath. Park in the road by the railway bridge.

Southdown
Fair sport with flounder on the flood tide. Use lugworm or ragworm. Best on spring tides. A useful mark after dark. Allow one hour over the published tide times, as the water takes a while to reach the upper reaches. Parking close by in the road.

Forder
Fish the early flood tide for flounder and school bass, using

king ragworm or lugworm. Fish at the mouth of the creek and move back with the tide. Crabs can be troublesome. A few parking spaces in the lanes near Antony Passage and railway bridge.

Blackpool Sands (nr. Dartmouth)
A fair mark for wrasse, pollack, bass; fish after dark for bull huss. Best on the flood tide. Use king ragworm, lugworm, soft crab and mackerel strips if after bull huss. Good parking space.

Bridport, West Bay Area
Bass, spurdog and pouting at night. Use fish baits for dogfish, otherwise king ragworm or lugworm. Whiting are taken at night during the winter months; some conger are taken at times. Fish the flood tide; best on springs. A good surf nearly always pounds the shingle. Mackerel roam close to the beach during the summer months.

Mevagissey
A variety of species are caught off the stone piers, including bass and mackerel which are usually caught by spinning or float fishing with a long thin strip of mackerel. Mullet roam the harbour on the flood tide. A tackle shop on the quay sometimes has live sand-eels. A very popular place during the summer months and parking is usually difficult, unless you are fishing by night or very early in the morning.

Lyme Regis (Dorset Coast)
Bass and at night bull huss and pouting; occasionally spurdog are taken. Use worm baits or fish baits for huss and spurdog. Best time to fish on spring tides. Fishes well after a good blow has disturbed the water. Mackerel come close inshore during the summer months, and are best caught by spinning with a silver spoon or toby lure.

Looe, Banjo Pier
Fish after dark when all is quiet, for big pollack, bass and dabs. Flounder are caught during the winter, casting across the mouth of the estuary. Use king ragworm, sand-eel or

lugworm. The flood tide is best and spring tides have the edge over neaps. Limited parking except after dark or in the early morning.

Prawle Point, nr. East Portlemouth
Big wrasse and a few pollack, on float tackle. The bottom is very bad and losses must be expected when bottom fishing, as this method seems to take the bigger wrasse. Use hardback or peeler crab and worm baits for pollack. The flood tide is best here.

Coombe Cellars, Teignmouth
Fish from the wooden jetty for good sized flounders on the flood tide. Best baits are peeler crab or soft crab; crabs are troublesome when using worm baits. Spring tides seem best at this mark.

Fowey Estuary
There are several marks where you can fish for wrasse, bass, thornback ray, and at night conger are taken to a good size. Fish the flood tide using peeler crab, sand-eel or king ragworm. For conger use fish baits, squid — or half a mackerel is as good as any.

West Hoe Pier, Plymouth
Mainly float fishing, but some bottom fishing, for many species including bass, wrasse, pollack, garfish and mackerel. At night, good sized conger are caught on ledgered fish bait. A whole small pouting can be good, and pouting can be caught from this pier after darkness. Use peeler crab or king ragworm. Some parking space on the main road, close to the pier.

Cofflete Creek
A mark for winter flounder fishing, on a rising tide; springs seem best. Some big bass have been taken here; occasionally whiting after dark, after a sharp frost. Crabs and sometimes eels can be troublesome when using worm baits. Follow the main Kingsbridge Road out of Plymouth up to Brixton village, and on the right you will see a pub called 'The Foxhound'. Take the road alongside this pub, signposted *Steer Point*;

follow down past the brick-works. It's a 'no through road' so drive right to the end — Cofflete Creek is on the right.

Puslinch
Another winter flounder mark on a flood tide at the very end of the Yealm. A few small bass and eels — which are a menace at night during the warmer months. Sea trout make their way up after April to join the river at Kitley. Use king ragworm or lugworm. Again take the Kingsbridge Road towards Yealmpton. Turn right at signpost marked *Newton Ferrers* for about half a mile until you come to Puslinch Bridge, where there is a freshwater river. On the right is a footpath through the woods; follow until the river ends and flows onto the mud flats. This is where you fish.

St. John's Lake
Fair flounder fishing during the winter months, nothing else seems to be caught here. Use king ragworm or lugworm. Spring tides are best. Follow the Torpoint Road from the ferry for approximately 1½ miles, then you will see a signpost on the left marked *St. John's*, take this turning. If you miss this turning there is another one on the left, a little further on.

Sedgwell Beach (Bigbury)
Mouth of the Bantham estuary. Cast sand-eel, king ragworm or lugworm for bass. Best catches are taken at night on a flood tide. Strong currents run on spring tides and weed can be troublesome after a period of rough weather. Good parking space in the main car park.

Challaborough Beach
A very popular beach during daylight, so fish after dark for bass and pouting. Best baits are king ragworm, lugworm, sand-eel, peeler crab and squid strips. Fair parking space at night.

Downderry Beaches
Fish the sand patches between the rocks for bass and plaice. Use king ragworm, lugworm or peeler crab. Fish the flood tide. Weed can be troublesome after a period of rough

weather. Some parking space in the road close to the shops.

Cargreen
Follow the main Callington Road until you reach a signpost on the right side of the road marked *Landulph*. Follow this road for some 1½ to 2 miles, then you will see a signpost marked *Cargreen* on the left side. Fish here for flounders during winter, using lugworm, king ragworm or peeler crab. Fair parking space at Cargreen.

Between Seaton and Portwrinkle
There is a good bass beach, fishing on a flood tide, but the bottom is bad and tackle losses are high. Wrasse are also taken at times. Use worm baits or crab. Poor fishing on a dropping tide and you must be prepared to spend at least six hours fishing at this beach, as you have to wait for the tide to drop enough to get back across the rocks. Best reached from the Portwrinkle end at low water.

Sandplace
A name given to this mark by local anglers — right opposite Seventeen Arches. Bass, flounders and eels are caught on worm baits. A place that fishes best on the flood tides and also springs. A long walk through Warleigh Woods to reach this mark, but the fishing can be good.

Saltash Pier and Waterside as far as Coombe Viaduct
Under the road bridge and the Brunel railway bridge there is a pier on the right where thornback ray are caught, and during a cold winter cod are taken here. Crabs are a menace when using worm baits, so ledger, peeler or soft crab. Strong currents run on spring tides and over six ounces of lead is needed to hold bottom. Parking close by the pier.

Up towards the viaduct we come to a small creek where, at the mouth, school bass and sometimes flounder can be caught, but the bass are on the small side.

Coxside Pier
Right opposite the Barbican, where the two small stone piers almost meet and the trawlers go through into Barbican

harbour. Float fishing will catch wrasse, pollack, and after dark small pouting. Use worm baits. Park in the square or alongside the rough road at Coxside.

Ballast Pond, Torpoint
A few school bass caught on worm or crab baits; after dark thornback ray, pouting and eels. Crabs are a menace when using worm baits. Fishes best on the flood tide, but strong currents run on spring tides and a fair amount of leads are needed to hold bottom. Fish from the harbour wall, but you must be prepared to stay until the tide drops, as the wall becomes surrounded halfway up the flood tide. Plenty of parking space in the road close to this wall.

Jupiter Point, nr. Torpoint
Some flounders can be caught all along the shoreline to the left. A few school bass are also taken on worm baits or crab. Very strong currents run on spring tides, and weed can then be troublesome. Some king ragworm can be dug at this mark, and plenty of weed hides many shore crabs. Good parking space close to the Point.

Hope Cove
Fish from the stone pier and cast across the beach for bass, using lugworm or sand-eel. Fishes best at night. Fish the flood tide. Local fishermen say conger are taken at night on fish baits. Limited parking close by.

Mothecombe Beach
Some bass are caught here, mostly at night. Use sand-eel, crab or worm baits. Best on the flood tide. Weed can be a menace and crabs are troublesome when using worm baits. Lugworm can be dug in the estuary at low water and plenty of sand-eels, if you are prepared to work for them. Limited parking in the road leading to the beach.

Cawsand
There are two beaches to fish from, for bass and wrasse, off the rocks. Too much activity in daylight with boats, so best to fish at night. Use worm baits and fish the flood tide; use crab for

wrasse. Again, limited parking space in the narrow roads.

Jennycliffe
Fish from the rocks for wrasse using float tackle — or ledger, if you are prepared to lose tackle. Use worm baits or crab. Best on the flood and spring tides. Good parking space in the car park close by.

Devil's Point
Wrasse and pollack are taken on mainly float tackle, using king ragworm. A very rocky area. Some very big wrasse are caught here at times; conger roam around at night and could be taken on fish baits. Plenty of parking space in the main car park.

Gara Beach, nr. East Portlemouth
Some good bass are caught from this beach on the flood tide, using lugworm or king ragworm. A hard climb down the cliff path to reach this beach. A few parking spaces on the cliff top close to Gara Hotel.

Freathy Beach (Whitsands)
Fair sized bass are taken here, but you must cast beyond the third breaker. A few plaice and turbot, caught on sand-eel or worm baits. Mackerel strip will also catch turbot. Fish the flood tide. Some parking space in the lay-bys on the road at the cliff top.

Palm Rock
Basically a winter mark for flounder and a few school bass. Some flounders run to well over two pounds. Best on the flood tide. Pouting are caught at night. Use soft crab or lugworm and king ragworm. Park in the road close by, just off the main road.

Renney Rocks
Giant wrasse are caught here using crab or worm baits. Fish the flood or ebb tide. You can float fish for them, but ledger is a safer bet. Be prepared to lose some tackle. You must spend up to seven hours or more on these rocks until the tide drops. Very occasionally some flat-fish are caught on the sandbanks.

Spider crabs in summer. Good parking space close by at Heybrook Bay.

Hallsands Beach
Fish the flood tide for bass, plaice, sole and turbot on thin strips of mackerel or sand-eel; after dark, pouting, whiting, rockling and a few dogfish on fish baits. Deep water close in. Use ledger tackle and worm or peeler crab. Good parking space close to the beach. Not a popular place, so usually plenty of fishing space.

Cotehele Quay
On the Callington Road close to Halton Quay. Small school bass, eels and a few flounders are caught on worm baits. Use ledger tackle and fish the flood or ebb tide. Good parking space right on the quay.

Stoke Beach (Main Beach)
To the East of Stoke Point there are many small sandy gullies and one main beach where small-eyed ray, pollack, conger and large wrasse are all caught from time to time. Fish at night for the rays and conger. Fishes best on a flood tide. For ray, use sand-eel and fish baits for conger; for wrasse use peeler, soft crab or king ragworm. Some degree of dedication is needed to catch fish here, but the fishing can be quite good. Some parking space on the waste ground close to the Co-op shop, before the caravan site.

Millendreath Beach
Fishes best at night when all is quiet, for bass and some congers. Fish from the stone wall to start with. Wrasse can be caught in the gullies during daylight. Use worm baits or fish for conger. Good parking space close to the beach.

Antony Passage
School bass and, during the winter months, some flounders can be taken on worm or soft crab. Fishes best on the flood tide. Lugworm and ragworm can be dug along this shore and peeler crabs are quite plentiful during the summer months. Parking in the road from Forder in a small lay-by.

PART II

PLACES TO FISH (FRESHWATER)

Heybrook Bay.

Stoke Point.

Rock Mark at Stoke Point.

Warleigh Point.

Wearde Quay.

Portwrinkle Pier.

Seaton Beach.

Coypool.

A sandy gully close to Mothecombe.

Plymbridge.

Rusty Anchor.

East Portlemouth, near Salcombe.

PLACES TO FISH (FRESHWATER)

Although my freshwater knowledge is limited, here are a few places that might help the beginner, and some dry flies that have proved successful for me.

Tavy
At Tavistock, brown trout and salmon. Some fast water and deep pools. Experiment with different flies, but for brown trout the black and peacock seems as good as any.

Plymbridge
Fishes well for brown trout, sea trout and salmon (fish at night for sea trout). Good dry flies are black and peacock spider, blue teal and the Alexandria. Fish above the falls for big sea trout and some salmon. Easy fishing and parking.

Clearbrook
Good fishing for sea trout and brown trout; occasionally salmon will take spinners. The mepps are very good. Good sized sea trout caught at night. Fish above the bridge; easy fishing but limited parking.

Goodameavy
Good fishing for brown trout and occasional sea trout, but for some reason difficult to tempt. Fish above the bridge. Good flies are black and peacock, red spinner, sherry spinner and blue teal. Easy fishing but limited parking by the bridge.

Burrator
Good sport can be had with rainbow trout, brown trout and brook trout. Useful flies are sherry spinner and red spinner; sometimes black and peacock spider. Easy fishing and good parking spaces. Use a fly with silver in it at night, like blue teal or the Alexandria.

Horrabridge
Fair fishing for brown trout. Some deep pools about a mile down river. Useful flies are black and peacock spider and sherry spinner. Easy parking but difficult fishing. A long walk to the best pools.

Bickleigh
Some very deep pools about one hundred yards up river from the bridge, that hold massive salmon, sea trout, and brown trout. Useful flies are thunder and lightning and blue charm; for trout, the black and peacock spider.

For all the above-mentioned places you will need a salmon licence, or a trout licence for trout fishing. As all of these rivers are club waters you will need a club water licence before fishing, which can be obtained at most tackle shops in Plymouth.

Looe Beach.

PART III

STORIES AND TACKLE TIPS

STORIES AND TACKLE TIPS

TACKLE TIPS

Twist round at least six times, make loop and put end back through loop, then pull tight.

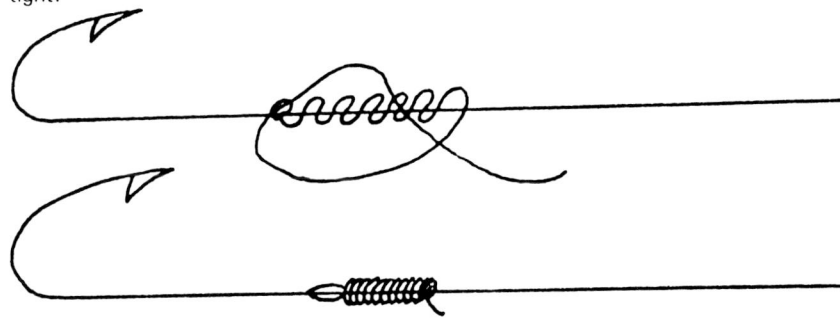

Finished — the perfect knot that won't slip. But you must remember to put end back through loop and pull.

A USEFUL KNOT

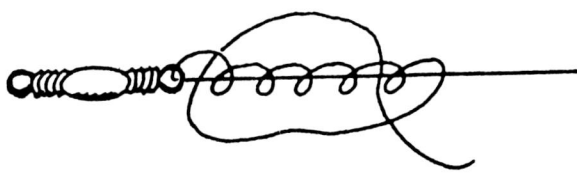

Put line through eye of swivel, twist at least six times. Put end through first twist loop next to swivel, then back through main loop and pull tight.

Finished knot that won't slip

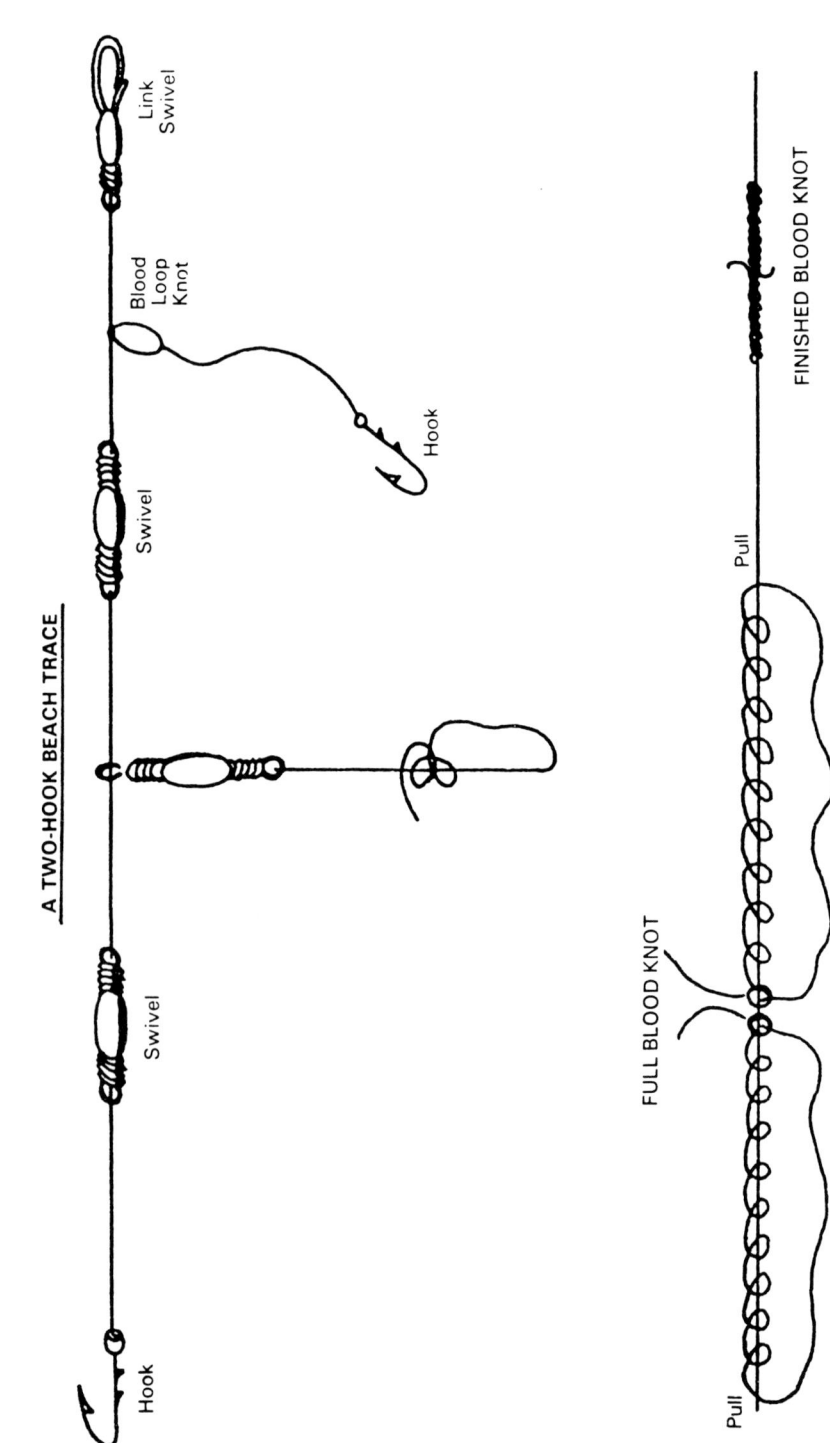

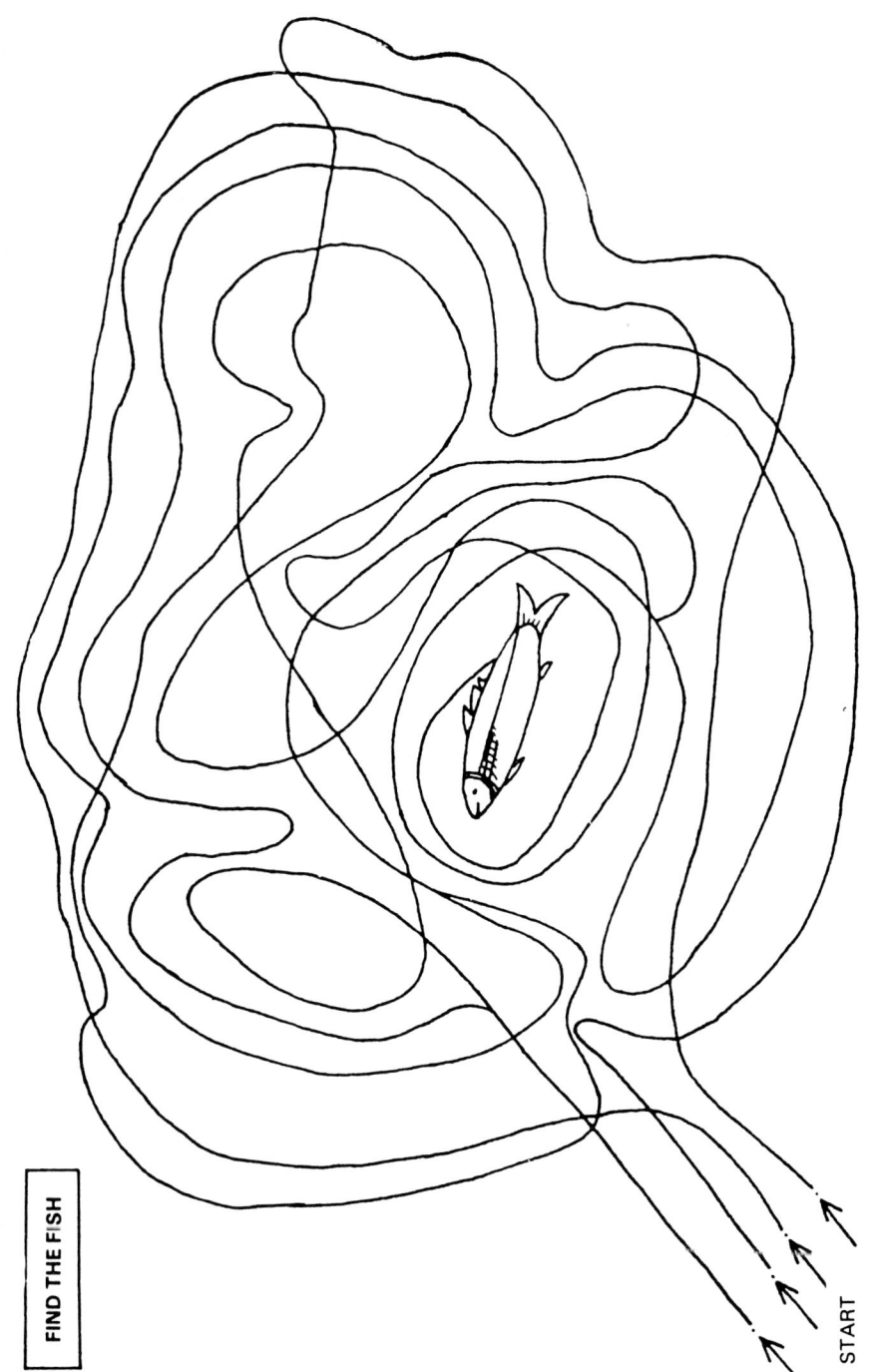

Fished at Heybrook Bay with Colin on the flood tide, a spring of 17·7, using lugworm and king ragworm, in daylight. The weather was dry but cold and the wind fresh north-westerly.

I tackled up a one-hook ledger, baited with king ragworm. Colin would float fish close to the bottom using lugworm. They were very slow at first; two hours had passed without a fish when I had a cracking bite. I struck hard and was into a good fish. I got him up off that terrible bottom fast and after he dived twice, I had him on the rocks: a nice wrasse about 2lb 8oz, which was what he weighed some time later. I slipped him into a rock pool and re-baited with two fresh king ragworm. Half an hour passed without any more bites and meanwhile Colin had changed to spinning tackle.

Then my rod banged over hard, I struck and was into a good fish which made a dive for the rocks, but I kept a tight line and after a struggle, landed a good wrasse bigger than my other one, which later weighed 3lb 10½oz and also went into the rock pool. I quickly re-baited with trembling hands, for this was good fishing. Out went my bait again into the kelp jungle. Colin had changed back to float tackle, but without any luck, and he was now using king ragworm.

It was close to high water when my rod dipped again. I waited, then came four hard pulls. A quick strike and he was on, but it wasn't a big one — about 1lb — and it was soon returned, unhurt, to the water. Colin still remained fishless, and we fished on for another hour, but we didn't catch anything more.

I was well pleased, with two very good wrasse. It was a great pity that Colin didn't catch anything before his return to Southampton the next day, but he said he had really enjoyed the last two days' fishing.

* * *

Fished at Renney Rocks (Heybrook Bay) with Jack Ashford on the flood and ebb tide, using peeler crab and king ragworm. The weather was dry, sunny and warm, the wind was light east to south-east, and the tide was a neap of 15·1.

This was our first time at Renney Rocks. It is way out into very deep water and can only be reached at low water, then you have to wait at least seven hours to get back again as the tide drops. We tackled up and Jack cast out — a long cast — but as the bottom is so bad I just dropped my bait into a gully straight in front of me. Jack lost his first trace, but on his second cast landed a small wrasse, which he soon returned. Some time later it was my turn and I landed a wrasse of about three quarters of a pound, which was quickly returned. Then it went dead for nearly one hour until my rod was nearly pulled out of my hands. I struck hard and a good fish dived for the rocks. I slowly pumped it to the surface after it made a few more runs, and I could see it was a very big wrasse — close to 6lb I would have thought. I slowly inched it to the net not daring to breathe, but I had him first time and the battle was won. I admired my prize.

Half an hour passed when Jack landed a tiny flat-fish, a small megrim in fact, but it was dead — it must have been on for some time. Then it was my turn again and I was into another big wrasse which again dived for cover, but I kept on the strain. I had to stop it reaching those rocks or it would be lost; but after what seemed an age, he was successfully landed. It was a huge wrasse, about 5lb I would guess. This was fantastic fishing. Would they keep this up? But no, it went dead for some time after that. I had a small pouting with me, so I cut him into small strips then lowered my bait back into the gully. Five minutes had passed when I had a few slight pulls, which went on for another five minutes so I struck and wound up. On the end was a spider crab, but as I got him close in, he dropped off back into the water and he was gone. Meanwhile, a skindiver appeared on the scene and soon found a big spider crab himself. He started swimming towards us and when he got close he asked me if I wanted the crab, so naturally I said yes. This then made up for the one I had lost a little while ago. We had run out of worms, so we had to use the crabs.

Another three hours passed without any more bites. By now the tide was on the ebb and we were thinking we would soon be able to get back across the rocks, when Jack's rod slammed down and he was into a decent fish which took some time to land. It was a wrasse of about four pounds; another good fish.

We fished on for one and a half hours without another bite

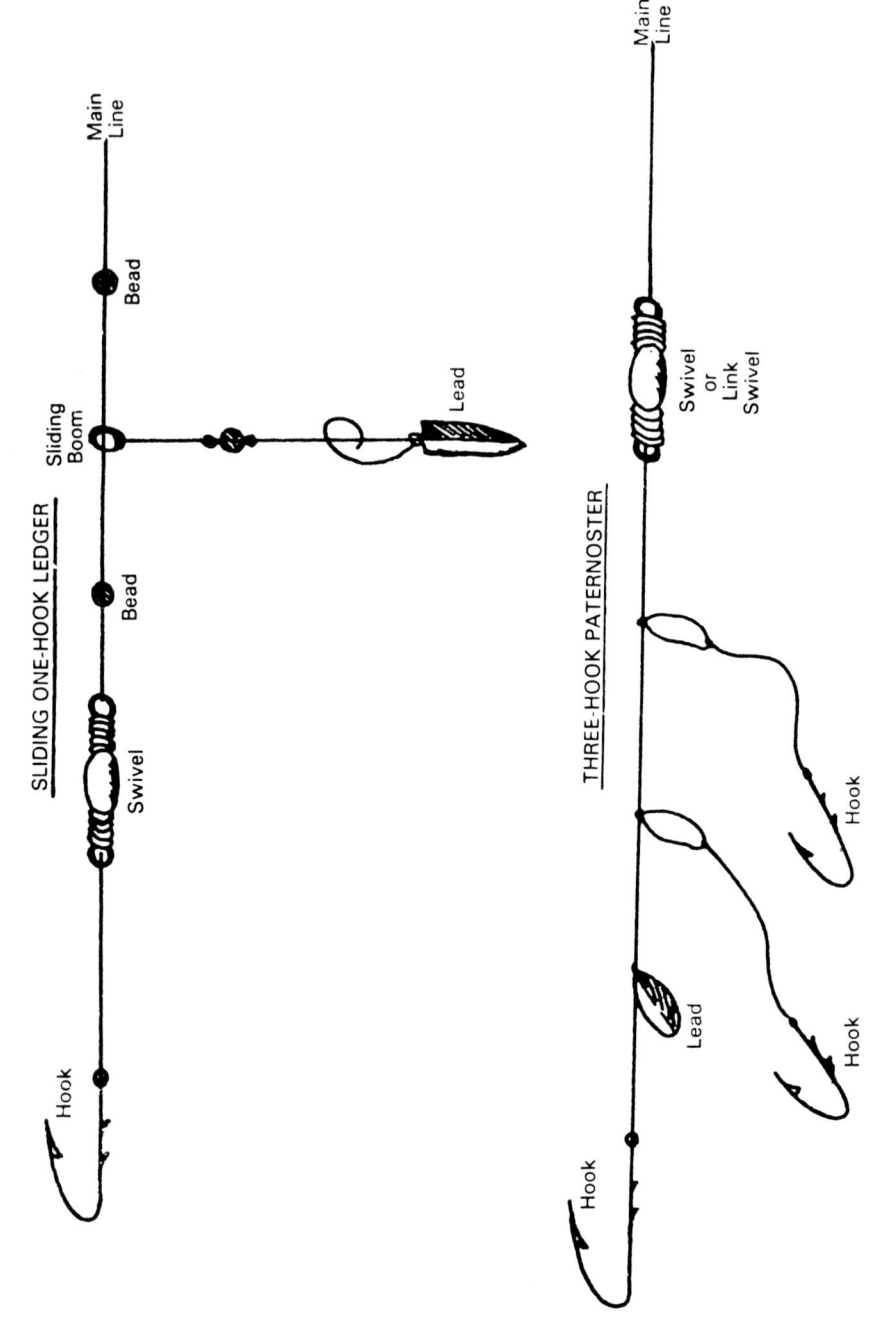

between us. By now we could just about make our way back, so I packed up first. Jack had another last cast but caught nothing more. We had been here for ten hours — we arrived at six o'clock and it was now four o'clock

TACKLE TIPS

For freezing long storage, sand-eels can be placed upright in coffee jars or jam jars. This way they will keep well for a considerable time.

Peeler crabs keep well placed in white petroleum jelly containers. They have a good tight screw on lid which seals out any smell.

Fished at Wearde Quay with Roger Palmer on the flood tide, a spring of 17-3, using king ragworm. We fished mostly in daylight, but for an hour after dark. The weather was cloudy but dry, the wind calm or light west to south-west.

We reached Wearde at the very start of the flood tide, so we tackled up two hooks with king ragworm. I was using twelve-pound line so I could cast further, and my first was close to 90 yards; Roger's went around 60 yards. Some ten minutes passed when my rod banged down hard and my line went slack, so I wound up and hit him hard and a good fish tore off to my right. I let him run and he soon turned and was running towards me. After a few minutes he was mine, a nice thick bass which looked close to 2lb — a good start. On went a fresh worm and a cast of 80 to 90 yards and twenty minutes later I was fighting my second bass, again a good one, around 1lb; a nice fish.

Meanwhile, Roger wasn't getting even a bite. He came over and admired my two bass, when my rod dipped again. I hit him hard and was into my third bass. This one was slightly smaller, close to three quarters of a pound, but a reasonable fish. On with another worm and I cast out again and waited, and it wasn't long before I landed my fourth bass — again, a nice fish, perhaps getting on for 1lb. This was fantastic fishing and I hadn't finished yet. I waited half an hour and again my rod dipped slightly. I waited, then it banged over

TACKLE TIPS

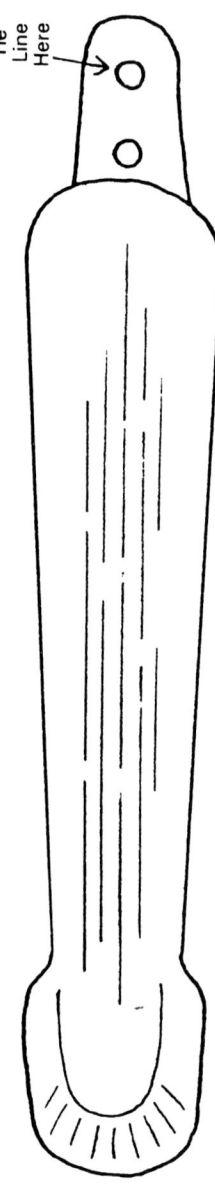

Tie Line Here

IDEAL fishing weights are metal stair carpet holders, found on both sides of stairs, which hold the carpet in position. Each one weighs close to 3oz. Good for fishing a rocky bottom, like Wrasse fishing.

OLD Yale door locks make good weights for a bad bottom.

TWO HOOK TANDEM STYLE
Ideal for presenting sandeel naturally

An effective way of hooking on a live sandeel hook once through the tail. Instead of the usual method most anglers use, through the top lip. Gives a firmer hook hold during casting.

BEACH ROD REST

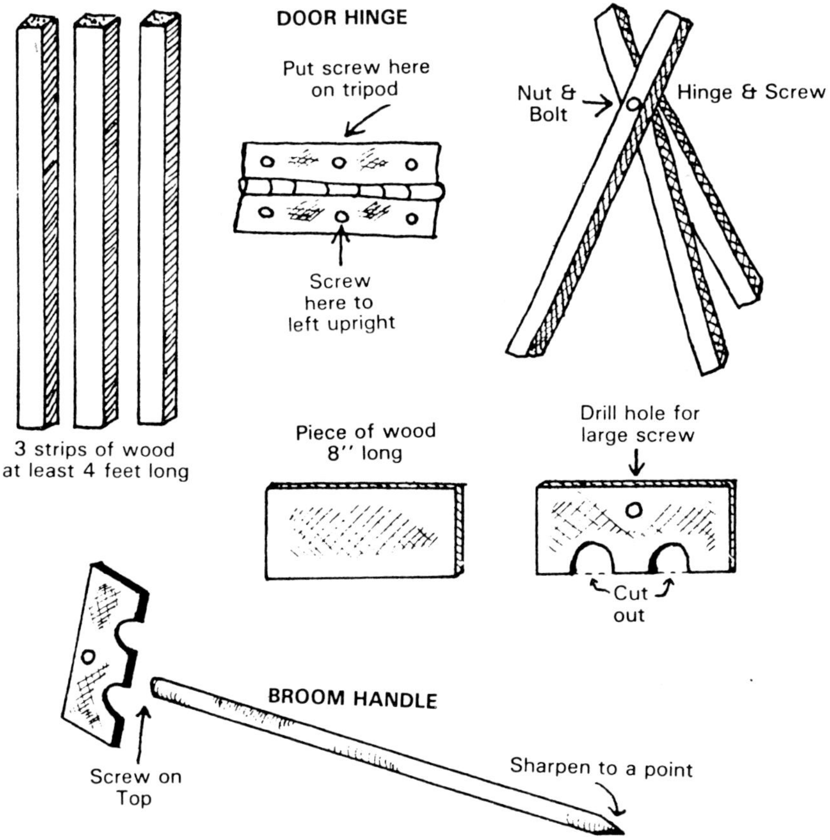

DOOR HINGE

Put screw here on tripod

Screw here to left upright

Nut & Bolt

Hinge & Screw

3 strips of wood at least 4 feet long

Piece of wood 8" long

Drill hole for large screw

Cut out

Screw on Top

BROOM HANDLE

Sharpen to a point

PLASTIC SPOON FOR FLOUNDER

Use the plastic medicine spoon for flounders. Snap off the handle (or cut off). Paint the spoon white, or any bright colour. Attach a split-ring through the narrow end, after punching a small hole.

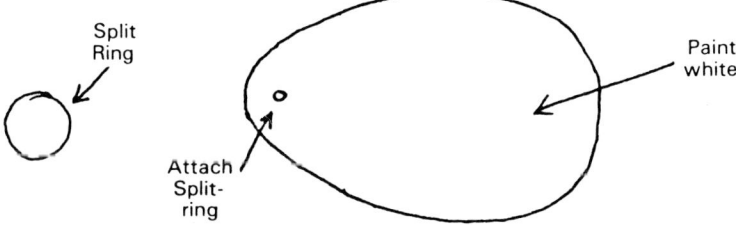

Split Ring

Attach Split-ring

Paint white

Flounder spoons can be made from the lids of ice cream tubs in the same way directed.

hard and a fish tore off down river towards the rocks. I put on side strain and managed to turn him and then he ran towards me. Two minutes later I had him — which gave me five bass.

Roger remained fishless until we moved onto the pier. My first cast produced a small pouting which I returned alive. Now it was Roger's turn and he soon landed a small bass which he returned; then he re-cast around 70 yards and soon had another bite. He waited, then came two harder pulls and he hit him hard and was soon fighting a good fish. It came easy for about 30 yards then dived for the rocks. I shouted to Roger, "Hold your rod up high and keep the strain on," but it was too late and was soon stuck fast. He pulled hard and the fish was lost; but some time later he landed his second fish, a small pouting. He had two more in the next twenty minutes, but they were small. Then at seven o'clock we packed up as I had to take Roger all the way back to Callington.

It had been a good night and I felt a warm glow of satisfaction when I again took another look at the super bass I had caught. A good catch had really sharpened my enthusiasm. All fish caught were returned, except my two-pounder.

* * *

Fished at Salcombe with Norman and Steve, from Friday night to Saturday morning. This time the weather was dry, but cold even for July; the wind was north-west then northerly and the tide was a spring of 17·3.

We arrived with two hours left of the flood tide and we quickly tackled up — it was still daylight. I cast a little to my left alongside the freshwater river, which was only flowing very slowly because we hadn't had any rain for weeks. I was holding my rod — in fact we all were, just in case they were biting fast — and five minutes later I had a cracking pull. I hit him hard and he shot off towards some rocks well up the beach, but I did manage to turn him away and very soon landed a 3lb mullet. Then it went dead for the next three hours.

It was now dark and there were only two hours left of the dropping tide. I then caught a school bass of 2¾lb. Steve and Norman then started getting school bass, and Norman also had a small dab. Then the bass stopped and in came the pouting, thick and fast; I caught five in ten minutes. Norman and Steve were also getting pouting, but they were small, hardly half a pound.

By now there was hardly any water, even in the main channel. It was nearly low water and it was two o'clock Saturday morning, so we packed up. We all had fish to take home and I was well pleased with the mullet I had caught on king ragworm.

* * *

Fished at the rock pile (near Bull Point) on the flood tide, a spring of 18-1, using king ragworm, in daylight. The weather was very stormy with heavy showers, some of hail, and the wind was storm force 10 westerly.

Conditions were very bad when I arrived at Ernesettle — huge breakers, white horses and very muddy coloured water — but I was very determined as I tackled up a two-hook paternoster and baited it with king ragworm. I cast out into the angry waters and waited. For the first hour I had a lot of problems with weed. Then I had a cracking bite which I saw even through the wind. I struck hard and a bass tore off up river. I soon managed to turn him and slowly brought him in closer; soon he lay at my feet, a nice bass close to 2½lb. I knocked him on the head and slipped him into the fish bag, re-baited and cast again into the teeth of the wind. I could only manage about 40 yards but I was still catching fish.

Some time had passed when my rod slammed down. I hit it hard and was soon fighting another bass. Again it went close to 2½lb — a nice fish! Into the fish bag he went. I baited-up with a fresh worm and cast again. By now the tide had become a lot deeper, the wind was even stronger and the breakers were reaching the top of the wall I was standing on, as it was a big tide (in fact it was becoming an angry torrent). Twenty minutes later my rod dipped then the line went slack; a quick strike and he was on, but he wasn't fighting much. In the shallows I could see it was a flat-fish; it wasn't a big one, about three quarters of a pound, but this gave me two bass and one flounder and it was still early in the tide. I should catch a few more yet; but the breakers were now breaking right over the wall and across the railway lines. I was getting soaked as the spray was also breaking over me.

Two more casts and then I had to pack up, as conditions were even worse and I was soaked. I didn't have any more bites, only two crabs, but I was well satisfied with three fish in the bag. The waters had been too rough today, but the fishing would be good when the storm died.

TACKLE TIPS
Unusual Baits

Baits that will catch fish in muddy rivers and estuaries:
Garden worms, ledgered in rivers like the Plym at Laira will take school bass, eels and some flounders.

I used to know a keen angler who used garden snails to good effect, without the shells, catching bass and a few mullet on quite large hooks.

Slugs have been known to work at times (if you can bring yourself to handle them).

Other unusual baits that can be used to good effect include sea slaters (sea lice), sand hoppers (if you can catch them), possibly woodlice (they look a lot like the sea slaters that are found on rocks).

Maggots for mullet could be worth a try, presented on a small hook and float (e.g. quill float).

Fished at Stoke Beach with Roger, on the flood tide, a neap of 15-7 — part daylight, part dark — using peeler crab, soft crab, live sand-eels and mackerel strip. The weather was mainly dry except for a little light rain and the wind was variable.

We walked down the hill from the car park, through the caravan site, down the ladder and across the beach for a mile and came to a long rock jutting well out to sea, which we elected to fish from. The tide was just on the turn as we tackled up our beachcasters with a long-flowing sliding trace. On one rod I put a live sand-eel hooked through both lips; on the other rod I put a nice big peeler crab (whole). I cast one rod straight out in front of me, the other to my left, into a sandy gully I had noticed earlier on. Roger baited two rods: one with sand-eel and one with mackerel strip, and cast both to his right and across the sandy bay.

Half an hour passed, during which time Roger lost a trace after casting too far onto the rocks. Then we sat on the rocks drinking a cup of coffee until his rod slammed down hard. He sprinted across the rocks and grabbed his rod, struck hard and was into a lively fish which fought hard; but after diving to the rocks twice, it was beaten and Roger landed a nice sized pollack — a good 2lb in weight — which he slipped into a rock pool after knocking it on the head. A good start and plenty of time for more yet. Twenty minutes later I missed a good bite; I had struck too late — it had taken crab bait — so on with a fresh crab and re-cast into the centre of the gully, just at the mouth.

It was a waiting game but I was rewarded some time later with a cracking bite. This time I was ready and hit it hard. A big fish dived for the rocks and my tackle went solid. I had two choices: I could keep on the strain or give him some slack line in the hope that he would think all was safe and the danger passed. I tried keeping a very tight line, but some minutes passed and he hadn't moved, so I let out some slack and he soon tore off out to sea.

I managed to stop him and turn him towards me. Again he dived for the rocks and I was stuck, but I got him moving again and once more he made it to the rocks below me. By now I was beginning to feel rather tired but I would not be beaten. On his next run he was rather slow, so I pumped him towards me. Roger was waiting with the net as I gently edged the giant fish towards the rocks, just below where we were standing. It was a very big wrasse, the biggest I had ever seen. "Must be 8lb," I said to Roger, as he slipped the net under him. It was a massive wrasse and as I weighed it on the spring balance it showed just under eight, a fabulous fish! I could not get back to have it weighed until morning, as we were now cut off by the tide, so I slipped it carefully into a rock pool along with Roger's pollack. This was good fishing. "We should do well tonight," I said to Roger, and he nodded.

"Seems like it."

We caught nothing more before darkness so I changed over to mackerel fillets on one rod, just in case there were any bull huss lurking around. The other rod was still baited with sand-eel. We waited patiently and settled down for a drink. We fished the tide all the way down, but the rods never moved; it was dead and we had to wait until dawn before we got back across the beach. The wrasse was so big that it would not go in my tackle bag, so I had to strap it on the top.

We weighed it on the scales when we got home and it was 7lb. 4oz, but it had lost a lot of weight. It was still a fabulous fish.

* * *

Fished at Portwrinkle (Finneygook Beach). It was my first time fishing here so I didn't know quite what to expect. It is a beach of golden sands but only 50 yards or so wide, with plenty of rocks on both sides (some of them covered with weed, so a good place for crab bait). There is also a small freshwater stream to the right which must be an attraction. I had king ragworm and mackerel strips for bait and I would fish the morning tide on the flood, a spring of 18-3.

It was now 3.30 a.m. High water was at 9.25 so I tackled up, then walked across the sands to the water's edge, which was a good two hundred yards out. I baited with king ragworm and then cast out around 80 yards. I had at least three hours to fish in darkness, so I had a good chance of a bass or two. My first bite came after some twenty minutes. I struck and landed a small pouting of hardly half a pound. I fished hard until daylight and had nothing more. I had a few bites but they were small and by now the tide had reached the lip of the beach, where there is a fairly deep pit — it would hold a good depth of water at high tide.

I was resting my rod when it was pulled hard twice, so I grabbed it, and struck and landed a good plaice which would at least give me something to go home with. I re-baited and cast out. Half an hour went by, then my rod banged down hard, so I struck and was into a nice fish which was fighting like mad. As I got him into the last two breakers I saw a flash of silver. 'A bass,' I said to myself confidently, but I was wrong and landed a very nice mackerel which had taken mackerel strip, and which later weighed 1lb 3½oz. This fish really made my day.

I fished for another hour without any more bites, so I packed up with three fish; but this beach was really worth another try some time. It had been raining hard earlier on, but had stopped just after I had got there. The wind was fresh north to north-west.

*   *   *

Fished at Heybrook Bay in my favourite gully, on the flood tide — a spring of 16-7 — using king ragworm, in daylight. The weather was stormy and cold; the wind was gale force eight, east to north-east — not the best of winds. Would it be like the old saying (I couldn't help remembering): 'when the wind's in the east the fish bite the least'?

I scrambled down the cliffs and slowly made my way towards my gully. The wind was howling straight into my face, there were huge breakers and plenty of white water coming in — and, of course, some weed as well.

I tackled up two rods, both with ledger one-hook tackle, and baited with two large king ragworms. I had spotted a deep, dark, almost black looking pool to my right, so I cast into the centre and waited. My other rod I cast just in front of me only 5 yards out, also into a deep gully.

I then fished on for quite some time before having my first bite and I struck hard and soon landed a 1lb wrasse. Then I had a few small touches for almost an hour; they were very slow, but then the rod jerked hard in my hands and I was soon fighting a lively wrasse, which was around 2½lb — a good fish. Then it went dead for almost one and a half hours until I had a cracking bite; I hit him hard and kept up the pressure. It was a good fish and as I got him close I could see he was a bass and a big one. He dived for the rocks several times but I wouldn't give any line. Six times he came to my landing net and I had to let him run again, but then he turned up on his side and I knew he was beaten. I carefully edged him, yet again, towards my net. This time I had him, and he lay at my feet. He looked a good 5lb and I was well pleased; I had a warm glow of satisfaction inside me.

I could have fished on, as I had plenty of bait left, but I packed up. I was truly satisfied. Who was it who said that about the north-east wind? Well, it couldn't have been a fisherman, could it?

PART IV

INSHORE BOAT-FISHING MARKS

INSHORE BOAT-FISHING MARKS

River Tamar Oil Jetties
Bass, thornback ray and pouting are caught alongside the pier; between two large round pillars there is a deep pit. Drop your bait into this pit. Use peeler crab or king ragworm.

Richmond Walk
A good mark alongside a floating marker the shape of a big barrel, close to the dockyard wall. Good sized pouting, wrasse, pollack and some black bream. Spider crabs can be caught on fish baits during the summer months. Use king ragworm or lugworm; both can be dug not far away from this mark at Admiral's Hard, from where the Cremyl ferry leaves.

Breakwater
A mile south of the breakwater there is a good mark. A few rocks on the bottom but good fishing. Pollack and mackerel with good sized pouting, mostly after dark. Use king ragworm or lugworm. For pollack, leave a good length of worm hanging from the hook point.

Wearde Quay
Just off Wearde Quay, some 200 yards out in the centre channel near the island, there is a good mark where thornback ray and bass can be taken and in winter, flounder, whiting and pouting. Use peeler crab or king ragworm.

Under Brunel Railway Bridge
Under the Brunel railway bridge, between the centre pillars, there is a deep pit where good sport can be had with bass, thornback ray, flounder, pouting and whiting. Sometimes cod show during a cold winter. Use peeler crab, king ragworm or lugworm.

Seventeen Arches
The centre channel at Seventeen Arches produces school bass, eels, mullet and occasionally thornback ray. During winter some whiting and pouting are taken on worm baits (winter, after dark), fish strip or peeler crab.

Landulph
One hundred and fifty yards out from Landulph produces thornback rays, eels and a few bass on king ragworm, lugworm or soft crab. Crabs can be troublesome when using worm baits.

PART V

YOUR BAIT AND WHERE TO FIND IT

YOUR BAIT AND WHERE TO FIND IT

Bantham Estuary
Sand-eel, lugworm
Mothecombe Estuary
Sand-eel, lugworm
Salcombe Estuary at East Portlemouth
Lugworm
Laira Embankment
Lugworm, ragworm
Millbrook Lake
Lugworm, ragworm
Jupiter Point
King ragworm, crab
Stoke Beach
Sand-eel
Seaton Beach (Cornwall)
Sand-eel, lugworm
Portwrinkle
Lugworm
Bigbury (Burgh Island)
Lugworm
Bovisand Pier (Harbour)
Lugworm
Wembury Beach
Sand-eel, lugworm
Blaxton Quay (nr. Lopwell)
Ragworm
Seventeen Arches
Lugworm, ragworm
Warleigh Point
Lugworm, crab, ragworm
Wearde Quay
Crabs, lugworm, a few king ragworm
Halton Quay
Ragworm
Coypool
Ragworm, a few peeler crab
St. John's Lake
Ragworm
Forder
Lugworm, king ragworm, soft and peeler crab
Shillingham Point
Lugworm, soft and peeler crab
Antony Passage
Lugworm, ragworm, soft and peeler crab
Ballast Pond
King ragworm, prawns
Admiral's Hard
Lugworm, king ragworm, ragworm, prawns
Millbay Docks
Prawns
Barbican
Prawns
Ernesettle
Lugworm, ragworm, clam, mussel, a few king ragworm
Bull Point
Lugworm, ragworm
Mud Cott Creek
Ragworm
Tamerton Creek
Ragworm
Maristow (Lopwell Dam)
Ragworm
Steer Point
Ragworm
Landulph Creek
Ragworm

PART VI

YOUR FISH AND WHERE TO FIND THEM

YOUR FISH AND WHERE TO FIND THEM

Wrasse (Ballan) (labrus bergylta)
A fabulous fighter. Fish for them at places like Stoke Point, mouth of the Yealm, Heybrook Bay, Bovisand rocks, Jennycliffe, Wembury, Devil's Point, Rusty Anchor, Millbay Docks, Burgh Island (Bigbury), the rocks near Thurlestone Beach, Blackpool Sands, Pottery Quay, Western Kings, Mutton Cove, Barbican, Portwrinkle, Salcombe estuary.

Baits: crab, worm, limpet or prawns.

Whiting (Merlangus merlangus)
A winter fish for the hardy angler. Found all around the coast of Devon and Cornwall. On the beaches or estuaries after dark.

Baits: fish baits, worms, prawns; even garden worms will catch these fish.

Weever (Lesser) (echiichthys vipera)
A lover of rocky ground, found around the coast of Devon and Cornwall, in places like Stoke Point, Wembury, Heybrook Bay, Rusty Anchor and Portwrinkle. A small fish, half a pound, would be a nice size.

Baits: worms.

Bull Huss (scyliorhinus stellaris)
A good fighting fish, taken at night at places like Stoke Beach, Slapton, Blackpool Sands and sometimes Thurlestone Sands. Caught mainly near rocks on ledger tackle.

Baits: fish baits.

Bass (Dicentrarchus labrax)
One of the most popular fish in the sea. A lover of rocky ground. Comes in close to the beaches after a storm has torn up the bottom. A very powerful fish, found all around the West Country; perhaps one of the best places to try your luck would be the Whitsand Bay area. A lovely fish to eat. They enter many of our rivers and estuaries like the Tamar, Lynher and Yealm.

Baits: worm, peeler crab, sand-eel.

Flounder (Platichthys flesus)
Mainly a winter fish in the West Country. Enters the rivers in November or December after a few sharp frosts. Found in the Tamar, Lynher and Tavy. Good places to try would be Palm Rock or Southdown, on the Millbrook Lake, Forder, Wearde Quay, Ernesettle Creek and places on the Yealm, Puslinch and Cofflete Creek.

Baits: worms, soft crab.

Pouting (Trisopterus luscus)
An easy fish to catch and find. You don't need special skills to catch pouting; a very underrated fish as they make a tasty meal. Found all around our coastline summer and winter. Best specimens are taken near rocks. Good sized ones are caught at places like the Barbican, Phoenix Wharf and Richmond Walk.

Baits: worms, fish strips.

Pollack (pollachius pollachius)
Another lover of rocky ground. A fine fighter on light tackle. Best method would be a small float and a large worm for bait, with the tail left hanging. Found all around our coastline. At night, fishing under a tilley gives good sport. Good places are Devil's Point, Millbay Docks, Stoke Point and Barbican.

Baits: king ragworm, lugworm, sand-eel.

Mackerel (Scomber scombrus)
Trawling has had a serious effect on the mackerel, and shore-fishing is only a shadow of what it used to be; but there are still some quite good places left, like Millbay Docks (for float fishing), Mutton Cove, Devil's Point and Rusty Anchor, and a few beaches where they can be caught on ledgered mackerel strip: Finneygook beach (Portwrinkle), Seaton Beach, Thurlestone and Slapton Sands (by spinning).

Baits: mackerel strip, garfish strip, spinners, toby lures, feathers.

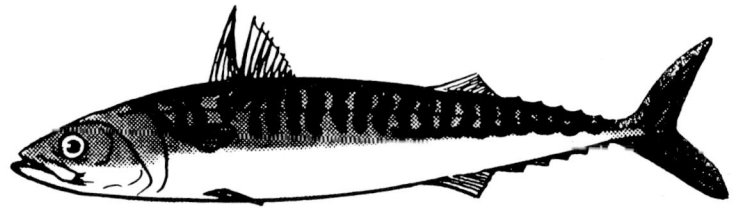

Small-eyed Ray (raja microocellata)
Found on a sandy bottom at places like Stoke Point, Mothecombe, Trevose Head, Whitsands and in the Yealm estuary at Season Point, Gara Point and Old Cellars beach. Night-time is the best time to fish for rays.

Baits: sand-eel, occasionally fish strip.

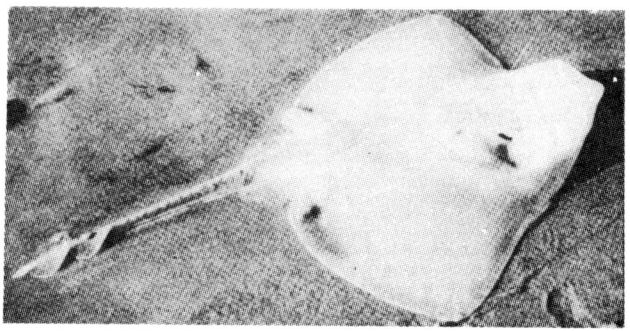

Thornback Ray (raja clavata)
Comes into the estuaries during late April. Another fish that has decreased in numbers due to extensive trawling, but can still be caught at places such as Cremyl beach (near Mashford's boatyard), Ballast Pond (Torpoint), Wilcove and Saltash pier (these are marks on the River Tamar). Sometimes they are taken from beaches in calm conditions. Stoke Beach is one such mark; another is Mothecombe and the River Yealm at Season Point and Old Cellars beach.

Baits: soft crab, peeler crab, can be taken on mackerel strips.

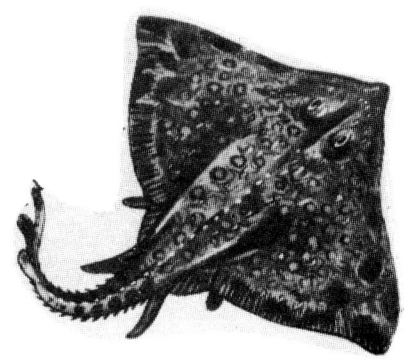

Conger (conger conger)
A fish of enormous strength, found over rocky, weedy ground. Found at many places around our coast such as Stoke Point, close to the rocks at Thurlestone, Seaton beach (Cornwall), Plymouth Hoe foreshore, Millbay Docks, Barbican, Wearde Quay, Mutton Cove, Western Kings and Rusty Anchor.

Baits: fish baits are the best, used as fresh as possible.

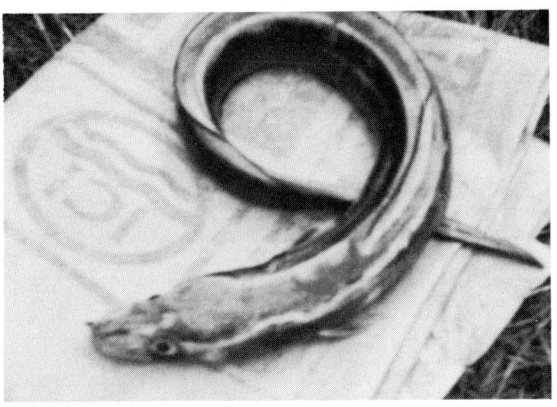

Garfish (belone belone)
A long slender-bodied fish, almost a miniature swordfish. Makes an appearance during the summer along with the mackerel. A fabulous fighter on light float tackle and a very small hook, baited with a long thin strip of their own kind or a strip of mackerel. Good places to try your luck would be West Hoe Pier, Millbay Docks and the Barbican. Comes close to the beaches during a calm spell.

Plaice (pleuronectes platessa)
Likes a sandy bottom. A fish mainly of the summer months, usually caught on small ragworm, king ragworm or lugworm. Some places to try would be Thurlestone Sands, Portwrinkle, Hallsands, Seaton beach (Cornwall) and a few at Ernesettle. A very pleasant tasting fish.

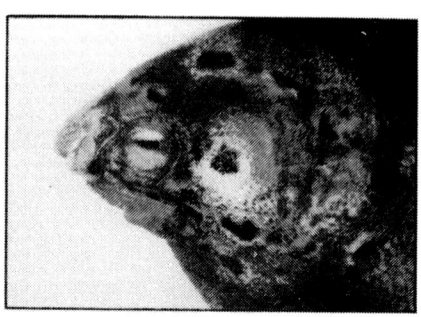

Turbot (scophthalmus maximus)
A lover of a sandy bottom. Best bait by far is a live sand-eel, but thin strips of mackerel or herring will work at times. Most shore fish seem to be on the small side, except when caught on night lines pegged out after dark. Good places to try for them are Whitsands, Portwrinkle, Hallsands and Slapton Sands.

PART VII

A GENERAL GUIDE TO SHORE FISHING IN THE WEST COUNTRY

A GENERAL GUIDE TO SHORE FISHING IN THE WEST COUNTRY, MONTH BY MONTH

January
A rather poor month for shore fishing, but good flounders to be found in the estuaries. Spring tides will give the best results. Use king ragworm or lugworm. Whiting at night.

February
Much the same as January, but some small school bass as well as flounders in the rivers. Again, spring tides are better. Whiting after dark.

March
A slight improvement and good-sized flounders. Some school bass and a few congers in the harbours. Night fishing gives the best results for conger, with fresh mackerel, herring or squid as bait.

April
A good month for shore fishing, particularly towards the end part. Bigger bass move in and thornback ray start to show. Peeler or soft crab is a must, early in the season.

May
Many of the summer species will now be showing up: bass, wrasse, pollack, conger, plaice, some mackerel and garfish. Dogfish at night. Thornback ray fishing should be improving all the time.

June
Summer fishing in full swing by now with a variety of species including bass, wrasse, mackerel, garfish, pollack, thornback ray, dogfish and conger.

July
Fishing should be improving all the time now and anglers should be enjoying fabulous sport off the rocks, beaches and estuaries, with all the usual species, plus mullet, dabs and turbot.

August
A good time to try for those big mullet. All the usual species still around. Good fishing at night for conger and dogfish.

September
An excellent month for big fish. Large wrasse off the rocks; big bass off many beaches; conger and small-eyed rays at night. Mackerel still around and good mullet fishing in the harbours. Pollack and plaice still present.

October
Another good month. Big bass, specimen wrasse found all around the rocky shoreline. A few plaice still on the beaches. Last chance to catch thornbacks before they move out. Dogfish and congers still present in numbers. Pollack fishing off the rocks.

November
Flounders start to make an appearance in the rivers. Some big wrasse still around if the weather is mild. Some congers off the rocks and dogfish at night.

December
Flounder fishing improving and after dark, whiting and pouting make an appearance. If the weather is very cold, a few small cod may be taken.

PART VIII

THE EFFECT OF
WEATHER CONDITIONS

THE EFFECT OF WEATHER CONDITIONS

Force 0
Calm. Bad conditions for beach fishing. Occasional good fish taken, mainly after dark.

Force 1
Light air. Again poor conditions.

Force 2
A light breeze. Again, rather poor conditions, but alright for inshore boat fishing.

Force 3
Gentle breeze. Slightly better conditions and a chance of a fish or two.

Force 4
Moderate winds and white horses. A good chance of a few bass.

Force 5
Fresh breeze. An ideal surf and a good chance of a decent fish or two, especially if the wind is from the south-west.

Force 6
A strong breeze. Getting a bit too strong for beach fishing; bringing in too much weed.

Force 7
A near gale. Plenty of white foam. Not good conditions.

Force 8
Gale. Very high waves. Best to stay at home until storm dies away, when good catches can be expected on the third and fourth tide.

Force 9
Severe gale. High waves and miles of white foam. Plenty of seaweed between the breakers. Best avoided until storm dies away.

Force 10
Storm force. A violent sea. Very high waves; white foam everywhere.

Force 11
Severe storm. Exceptionally high waves; bad visibility.

Force 12
Hurricane. Sea becomes completely covered in white foam. Again, exceptionally high breakers; the sea is a mass of weed.

PART IX

MAPS

A GENERAL GUIDE TO MAIN PLACES DESCRIBED

(1) SLAPTON
(2) EAST PORTLEMOUTH
(3) BANTHAM
(4) THURLESTONE SANDS
(5) BIGBURY/CHALLABOROUGH
(6) WEMBURY
(7) HEYBROOK BAY
(8) BOVISAND
(9) PORTWRINKLE/FINNEYGOOK
(10) SEATON
(11) STOKE BEACH/POINT
(12) TREGANTLE/TREGONHAWKE
(13) HARLYN BAY
(14) PICKLECOMBE PIER
(15) BLACKPOOL SANDS

ALL OTHER PLACES MENTIONED ARE IN THE PLYMOUTH AREA EXCEPT SOUTHDOWN WHICH IS ON MILLBROOK LAKE, AS IS PALM ROCK. FORDER, SHILLINGHAM AND WEARDE QUAY, ARE MARKS ON THE RIVER LYNHER, WILCOVE, BRUNEL GREEN, HALTON QUAY AND LANDULPH ARE MARKS ON THE RIVER TAMAR, AND STEER POINT IS ON THE RIVER YEALM, AS IS PUSLINCH AND COFFLETE.
COOMBE CELLARS IS ON THE RIVER TEIGN.

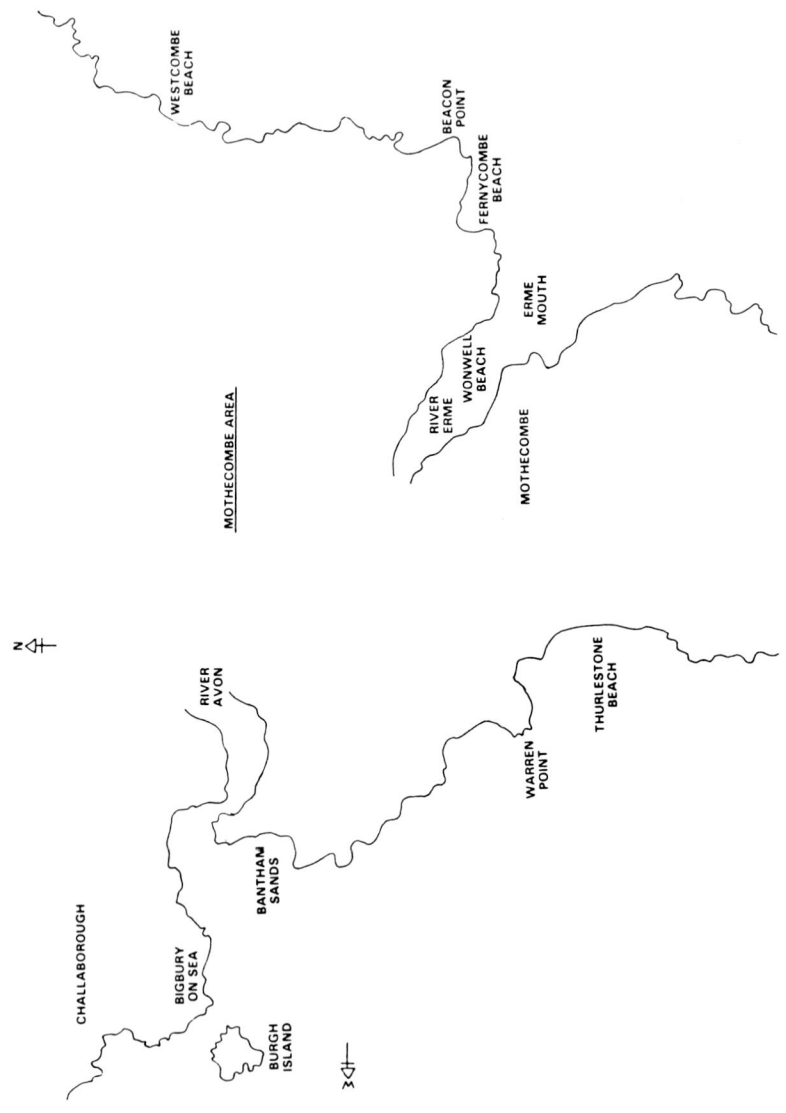

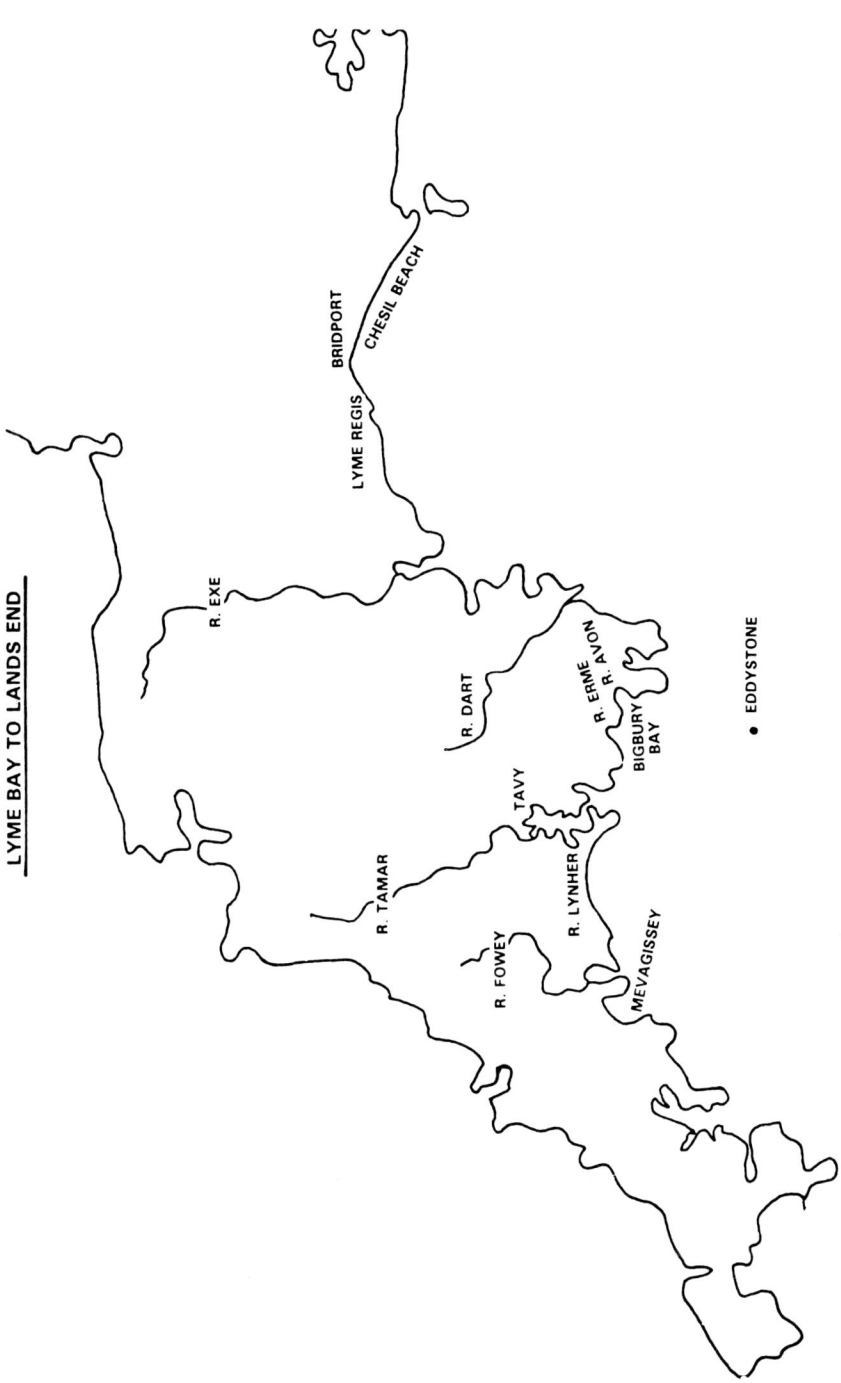

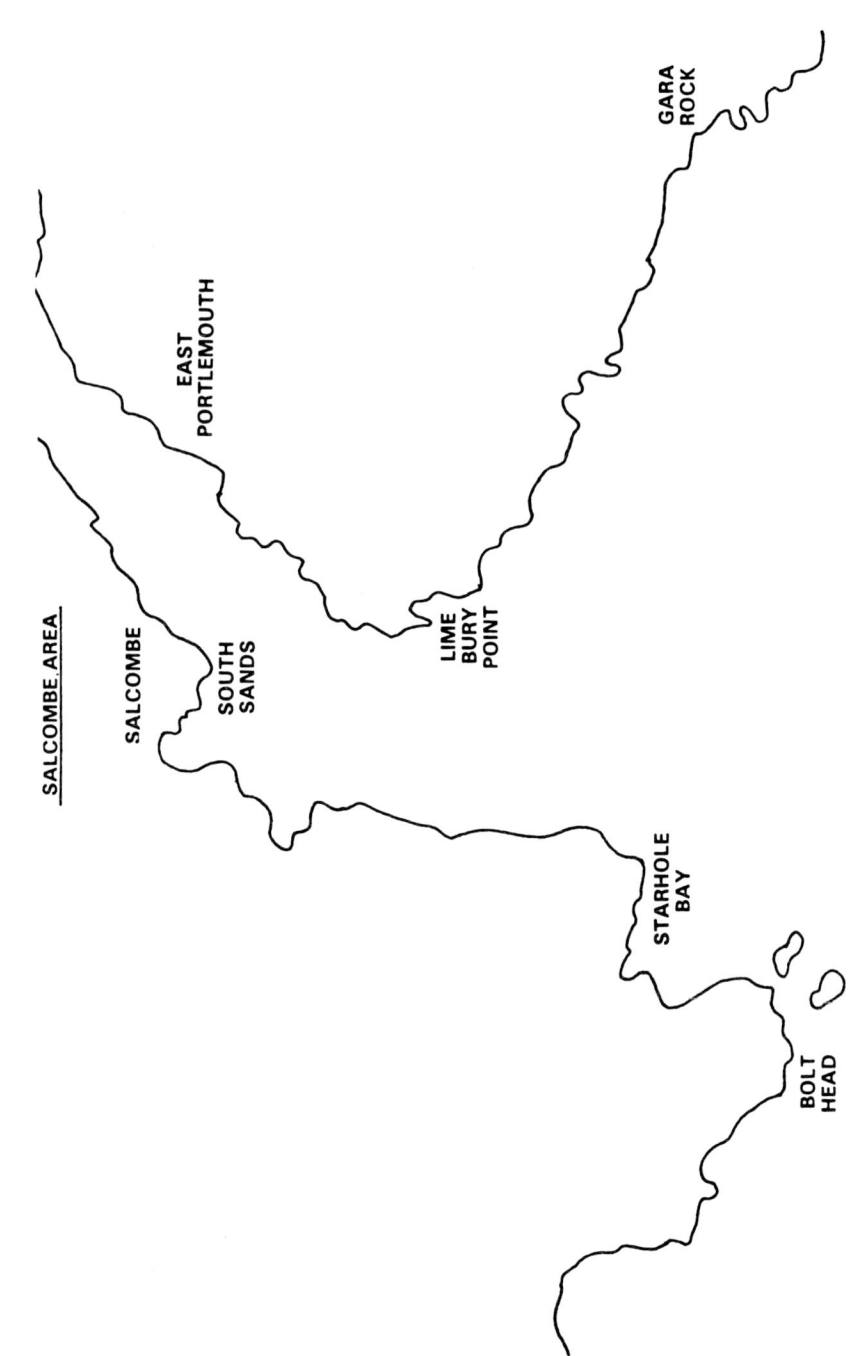

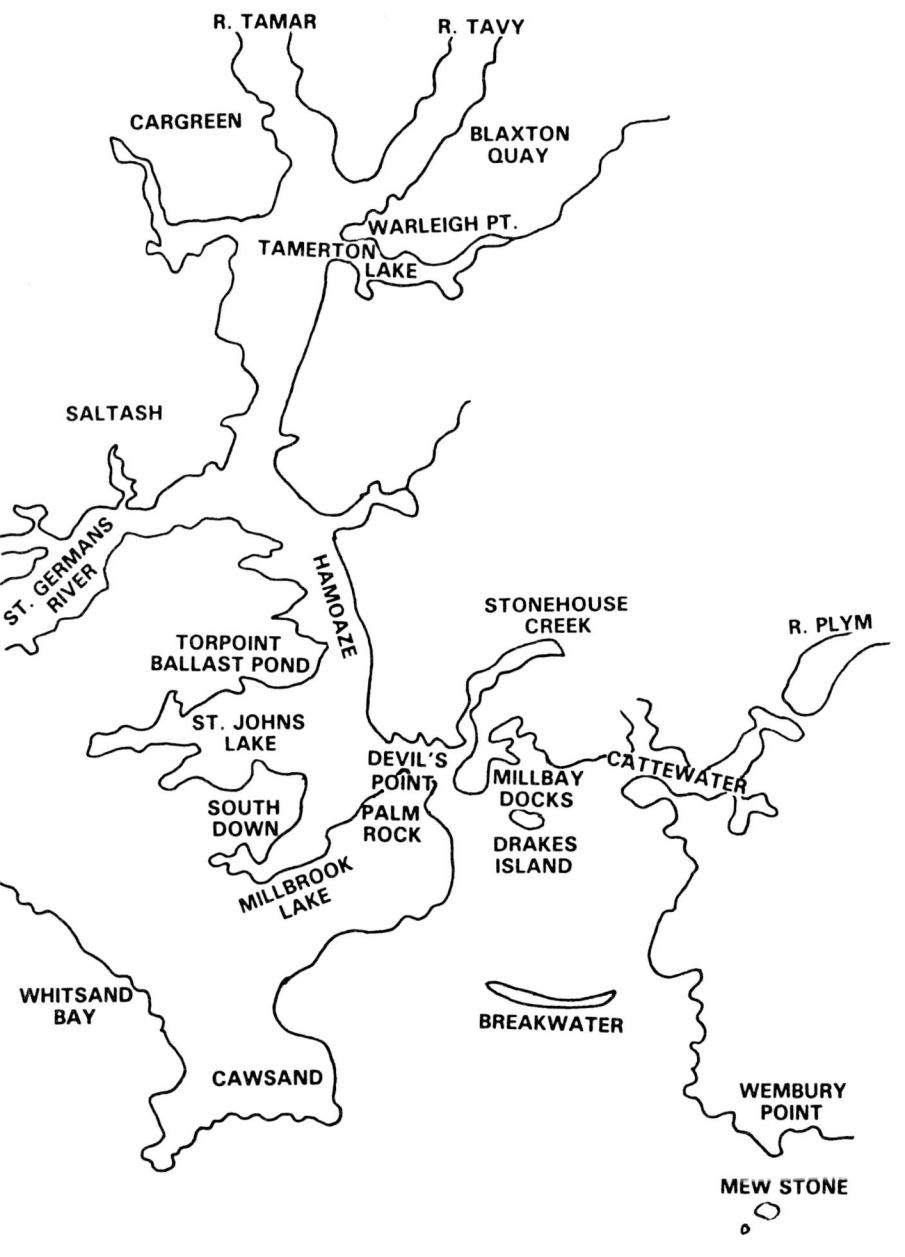

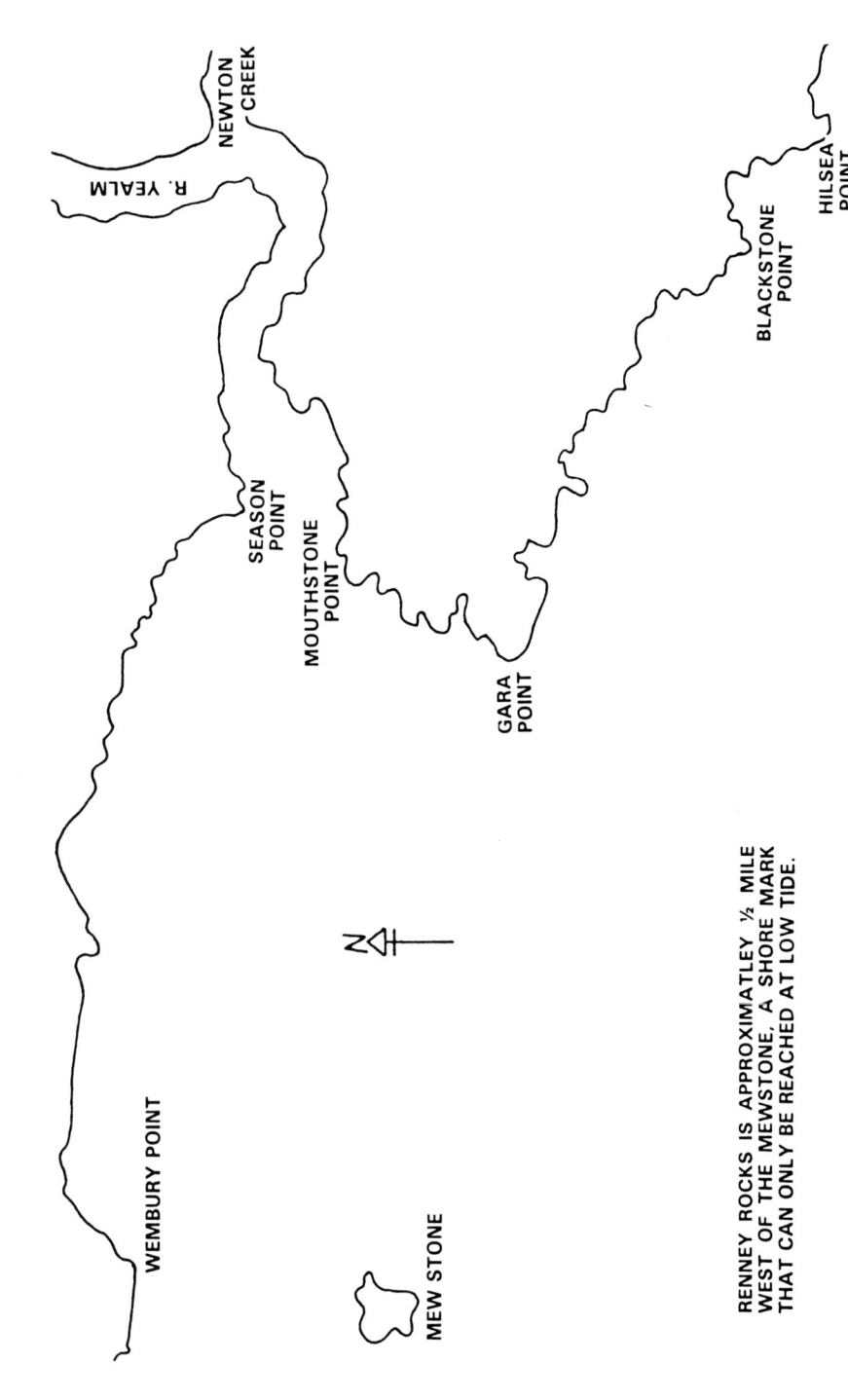

PART X

QUIZWORDS

QUIZWORDS

Hidden in the grid are the names of all the fish listed below. The names can run horizontally, vertically or diagonally, backwards or forwards, but all the words will be in a straight line. Put a line through the ones you can find. Some letters will be used more than once, and some will not be used at all. GOOD LUCK!

E	E	L	D	O	B	P	M	W	U	K	Y	A
L	D	M	B	E	L	O	W	U	Y	S	A	D
T	H	B	M	U	L	L	E	T	C	W	R	O
F	S	G	M	P	C	L	K	D	M	U	W	G
L	W	B	S	R	O	A	O	C	D	W	Y	F
O	H	I	L	K	O	C	O	N	G	E	R	I
U	N	E	G	C	S	K	F	I	L	E	T	S
N	H	I	F	O	W	F	L	R	A	L	E	H
D	E	S	H	D	I	R	W	L	O	U	B	D
E	O	L	L	D	S	C	A	O	D	R	H	I
R	M	P	W	A	F	R	O	S	U	H	F	I
G	L	M	B	H	M	U	L	R	S	W	C	O
S	B	A	S	S	Y	S	E	L	F	E	I	H

COD, BASS, FLOUNDER, CONGER, DOGFISH, EEL, HADDOCK, POLLOCK, MULLET, RAY, WRASSE

In the following quizwords all the names listed are hidden. They may run forwards or backwards, horizontally, vertically or diagonally, but always in a straight line. Some letters may be used more than once and some may not be used at all.

91

1. FIND THE BAIT

K	L	I	M	P	E	T	H	C	D	M	O	M	I	T
C	B	M	A	C	K	H	G	L	D	O	F	E	B	A
M	C	D	C	B	O	N	L	G	H	P	M	L	T	X
T	V	Q	K	W	I	L	X	Y	R	Z	M	K	L	C
R	M	P	E	R	T	X	F	A	Z	X	R	C	Q	R
A	W	V	R	S	F	L	W	L	B	C	O	O	L	A
G	V	E	E	Y	Z	N	X	I	G	J	W	C	E	B
W	H	K	L	E	S	S	U	M	C	M	G	O	E	T
O	P	R	S	L	X	Q	V	W	L	A	U	M	D	U
R	S	P	A	B	C	L	I	M	C	K	L	Z	N	Q
M	R	P	V	R	Y	J	P	Q	Z	X	L	F	A	B
P	R	M	U	E	S	I	J	X	Z	P	H	U	S	T
T	A	P	M	A	L	C	Z	Q	V	W	R	E	A	D
S	Q	U	I	D	B	V	G	N	I	T	U	O	P	T

CRAB, LIMPET, SANDEEL, LUGWORM, MUSSEL, CLAM, COCKLE, BREAD, RAGWORM, PRAWN, SQUID, MACKEREL, HERRING, POUTING

2. FIND THE EQUIPMENT

D	C	B	E	R	O	D	K	H	N	E	L	A	I
K	O	R	T	C	H	C	D	T	L	O	M	L	T
L	M	E	C	H	O	P	C	A	M	T	P	O	I
E	T	E	L	E	O	L	F	L	O	A	T	C	T
A	P	L	K	N	K	M	K	H	P	D	B	L	T
D	L	M	K	I	S	T	W	A	D	E	R	S	P
L	P	T	N	L	T	E	N	S	D	R	P	S	T
F	L	M	T	C	L	S	W	I	V	E	L	S	P
F	C	L	B	D	P	S	P	V	L	K	B	S	T
A	C	R	B	I	L	D	K	B	V	C	I	R	L
K	L	M	N	O	T	P	N	K	O	P	L	B	D
C	B	N	O	T	R	E	C	D	M	P	T	L	C
L	E	P	N	E	R	B	T	I	A	B	L	P	T
R	R	E	G	R	O	G	S	I	D	C	N	M	O

ROD, REEL, HOOKS, LEAD, LINE, FLOAT, SPINNER, WADERS, NET, GAFF, SWIVELS, BEADS, BAIT, DISGORGER

3. FIND THE RIVER

L	Y	X	C	V	P	L	Y	M	B	A	L	T
Y	N	C	I	N	N	Y	D	L	P	Q	X	Y
T	A	Y	V	A	T	C	B	L	P	X	Z	Y
L	P	M	N	T	A	M	C	R	R	P	Y	E
E	P	L	A	E	B	D	F	G	A	L	P	A
M	C	V	X	T	R	Y	L	P	M	G	H	L
A	B	M	G	N	Z	M	Y	P	A	H	E	M
C	O	L	O	T	M	P	E	Z	T	L	Y	H
M	A	V	F	M	W	P	E	Y	L	T	M	H
C	A	Z	E	L	Y	N	H	E	R	P	Y	T
F	G	A	M	T	E	F	W	C	A	M	T	P
H	V	L	A	C	M	M	A	H	K	L	A	W
Y	C	V	Z	Y	E	W	O	F	X	C	L	T

PLYM, YEALM, TAMAR, TAVY, LYNHER, MEAVY, WALKHAM. INNY, FOWEY, CAMEL, AVON, ERME

4. FIND THE FISHING PLACE

C	B	A	N	A	C	I	B	R	A	B	L	T	G
F	I	T	H	U	M	S	E	A	T	O	N	N	E
F	G	E	B	M	O	C	L	A	S	S	J	J	S
W	B	X	C	L	Y	T	F	W	C	A	E	M	D
H	V	T	B	O	V	T	E	L	D	N	D	O	N
I	R	P	T	A	R	M	M	L	N	T	N	T	A
T	Y	L	T	A	B	A	B	Y	A	S	A	H	S
S	A	N	T	U	H	B	C	N	S	T	S	E	L
A	X	Z	R	T	L	L	W	O	W	I	I	C	L
N	X	Y	N	T	I	C	H	T	A	B	V	O	A
D	B	A	F	F	L	E	U	P	C	O	O	M	H
S	B	A	F	X	H	O	J	A	O	T	B	B	T
P	Q	E	S	E	A	O	F	L	P	Q	R	E	T
S	X	T	H	U	R	L	E	S	T	O	N	E	P

SLAPTON, SALCOMBE, WEMBURY, HALLSANDS, BARBICAN, WHITSANDS, SEATON, JENNYCLIFFE, BOVISAND, BANTHAM, BIGBURY, MOTHECOMBE, LOOE, THURLESTONE, CAWSAND

THE LUCKLESS ANGLER

A typical angler, loaded up with everything but the kitchen sink — new rod, reel, waders, gaff, net, tilley lamp and a flask of hot coffee — struggles down to the beach, tackles up, takes ten minutes to thread on a worm after losing a couple and pricks his finger twice on the hook point. Marches down the beach, heaves out his line with an almighty throw and sends his end tackle out 200 yards, but without the main line. On with a new trace, charges down the beach, and slips on a patch of weed, falling face first into the water. He murmurs to himself, then is soon off again. This time the trace goes one way and the bait flies off the other way. He throws his rod on the sand then sits down for a drink from his flask, calms himself and then he's off again, but soon runs out of traces. He then has to pack up in disgust, never to fish again.